The Office U.S.

MAD LIBS

by Brian Elling
and Alexandra L. Wolfe

MAD LIBS
An imprint of Penguin Random House LLC, New York

First published in the United States of America by Mad Libs,
an imprint of Penguin Random House LLC, New York, 2021

Mad Libs format copyright © 2021 by Penguin Random House LLC

Concept created by Roger Price & Leonard Stern

© 2021 Universal Television LLC. All Rights Reserved.

MAD LIBS and logo are registered trademarks of Penguin Random House LLC.

Visit us online at penguinrandomhouse.com.

Printed in the United States of America

ISBN 9780593226759
1 3 5 7 9 10 8 6 4 2
CW

MAD LIBS®
INSTRUCTIONS

MAD LIBS® is a game for people who don't like games! It can be played by one, two, three, four, or forty.

• RIDICULOUSLY SIMPLE DIRECTIONS

In this tablet you will find stories containing blank spaces where words are left out. One player, the READER, selects one of these stories. The READER does not tell anyone what the story is about. Instead, he/she asks the other players, the WRITERS, to give him/her words. These words are used to fill in the blank spaces in the story.

• TO PLAY

The READER asks each WRITER in turn to call out a word—an adjective or a noun or whatever the space calls for—and uses them to fill in the blank spaces in the story. The result is a MAD LIBS® game.

When the READER then reads the completed MAD LIBS® game to the other players, they will discover that they have written a story that is fantastic, screamingly funny, shocking, silly, crazy, or just plain dumb—depending upon which words each WRITER called out.

• EXAMPLE (*Before* and *After*)

" _____ !" he said _____
  EXCLAMATION   ADVERB

as he jumped into his convertible _____ and
                                          NOUN

drove off with his _____ wife.
                         ADJECTIVE

" _____OUCH_____ !" he said _____HAPPILY_____
      EXCLAMATION   ADVERB

as he jumped into his convertible _____CAT_____ and
                                          NOUN

drove off with his _____BRAVE_____ wife.
                         ADJECTIVE

MAD LIBS
QUICK REVIEW

In case you have forgotten what adjectives, adverbs, nouns, and verbs are, here is a quick review:

An ADJECTIVE describes something or somebody. *Lumpy*, *soft*, *ugly*, *messy*, and *short* are adjectives.

An ADVERB tells how something is done. It modifies a verb and usually ends in "ly." *Modestly*, *stupidly*, *greedily*, and *carefully* are adverbs.

A NOUN is the name of a person, place, or thing. *Sidewalk*, *umbrella*, *bridle*, *bathtub*, and *nose* are nouns.

A VERB is an action word. *Run*, *pitch*, *jump*, and *swim* are verbs. Put the verbs in past tense if the directions say PAST TENSE. *Ran*, *pitched*, *jumped*, and *swam* are verbs in the past tense.

When we ask for A PLACE, we mean any sort of place: a country or city (*Spain*, *Cleveland*) or a room (*bathroom*, *kitchen*).

An EXCLAMATION or SILLY WORD is any sort of funny sound, gasp, grunt, or outcry, like *Wow!*, *Ouch!*, *Whomp!*, *Ick!*, and *Gadzooks!*

When we ask for specific words, like a NUMBER, a COLOR, an ANIMAL, or a PART OF THE BODY, we mean a word that is one of those things, like *seven*, *blue*, *horse*, or *head*.

When we ask for a PLURAL, it means more than one. For example, *cat* pluralized is *cats*.

MAD LIBS® is fun to play with friends, but you can also play it by yourself! To begin with, DO NOT look at the story on the page below. Fill in the blanks on this page with the words called for. Then, using the words you have selected, fill in the blank spaces in the story.

Now you've created your own hilarious MAD LIBS® game!

MICHAEL'S LEADERSHIP PHILOSOPHY

OCCUPATION _____

ADJECTIVE _____

VERB _____

ADVERB _____

VERB _____

VERB ENDING IN "ING" _____

OCCUPATION _____

NOUN _____

PLURAL NOUN _____

NUMBER _____

OCCUPATION _____

ADJECTIVE _____

LAST NAME _____

SOMETHING ALIVE _____

EXCLAMATION _____

SAME EXCLAMATION _____

VERB _____

VERB (PAST TENSE) _____

People say I am the best _____. They go, "We've never

OCCUPATION

worked in a place like this before. You're _____, and you

ADJECTIVE

_____ the best out of us." At Dunder Mifflin, we work

VERB

_____, we _____ hard. Sometimes we play hard

ADVERB   VERB

when we should be _____ hard. I guess the atmosphere

VERB ENDING IN "ING"

that I've created here is that I'm a friend first, and a/an _____

OCCUPATION

second . . . and probably an entertainer third. After all, what is the most

important thing for a company? Is it the _____-flow? Is it

NOUN

the inventory? Nuh-uh. It's the _____. My proudest

PLURAL NOUN

moment here was not when I increased profits by _____

NUMBER

percent or when I cut expenses without losing a single _____.

OCCUPATION

No, no, no, no, no. It was a/an _____ guy. He came to me,

ADJECTIVE

and said, "Mr. _____, would you be the godfather of my

LAST NAME

_____?" _____. _____. Too bad

SOMETHING ALIVE   EXCLAMATION   SAME EXCLAMATION

it didn't work out in the end. We had to let him _____. He

VERB

_____.

VERB (PAST TENSE)

MAD LIBS® is fun to play with friends, but you can also play it by yourself! To begin with, DO NOT look at the story on the page below. Fill in the blanks on this page with the words called for. Then, using the words you have selected, fill in the blank spaces in the story.

Now you've created your own hilarious MAD LIBS® game!

KEVIN'S FAMOUS CHILI

VERB ENDING IN "S" _____

SILLY WORD _____

NOUN _____

ADJECTIVE _____

NOUN _____

VERB _____

ADJECTIVE _____

VERB _____

TYPE OF FOOD _____

TYPE OF CONTAINER _____

ADJECTIVE _____

VERB ENDING IN "ING" _____

TYPE OF FOOD (PLURAL) _____

ADJECTIVE _____

NOUN _____

LAST NAME (PLURAL) _____

NOUN _____

MAD LIBS

KEVIN'S FAMOUS CHILI

Kevin loves to make his famous chili for everyone who

_____ at Dunder _____ . I just hope he
VERB ENDING IN "S"   SILLY WORD

doesn't spill it on the _____ this year. Here's what he had to
                              NOUN

say about his _____ recipe:
                   ADJECTIVE

"At least once a/an _____ , I like to _____ in some of
                        NOUN   VERB

my Kevin's _____ Chili. The trick is to under-_____
              ADJECTIVE   VERB

the _____ . Everybody is going to get to know each other in
       TYPE OF FOOD

the _____ . I'm _____ about this stuff. I'm
       TYPE OF CONTAINER   ADJECTIVE

up the night before _____ garlic and dicing whole
                        VERB ENDING IN "ING"

_____ . I toast my own _____ chilies. It's
TYPE OF FOOD (PLURAL)   ADJECTIVE

a/an _____ passed down from _____ for
          NOUN   LAST NAME (PLURAL)

generations. It's probably the _____ I do best."
                                   NOUN

MAD LIBS® is fun to play with friends, but you can also play it by yourself! To begin with, DO NOT look at the story on the page below. Fill in the blanks on this page with the words called for. Then, using the words you have selected, fill in the blank spaces in the story.

Now you've created your own hilarious MAD LIBS® game!

THE DUNDIES

NOUN _____

VERB (PAST TENSE) _____

OCCUPATION (PLURAL) _____

NOUN _____

PERSON IN ROOM _____

TYPE OF BUILDING _____

NUMBER _____

NOUN _____

OCCUPATION _____

PART OF THE BODY _____

SILLY WORD _____

SAME SILLY WORD _____

NOUN _____

ADJECTIVE _____

VERB ENDING IN "ING" _____

NOUN _____

VERB ENDING IN "ING" _____

NOUN _____

MAD LIBS®

THE DUNDIES

_____-roll, please! The list of the fourteenth annual Dundie
         NOUN

Award winners has been _____ . Congratulations to all
                              VERB (PAST TENSE)

our _____:
      OCCUPATION (PLURAL)

Jim: Best _____ Award
                  NOUN

_____: Best Mom Award
  PERSON IN ROOM

Ryan Howard: Hottest in the _____ Award for Over
                                      TYPE OF BUILDING

_____ Years
    NUMBER

Stanley: _____ Award
                  NOUN

Dwight: Promising Assistant _____ Award
                                     OCCUPATION

Erin: Cutest Red-_____ in the Office Award
                       PART OF THE BODY

Andy: _____, _____ _____-head of the
            SILLY WORD   SAME SILLY WORD   NOUN

Year Award

Toby: _____ Repulsiveness Award
              ADJECTIVE

Phyllis: _____ Beauty Award
               VERB ENDING IN "ING"

Angela: Kind of a/an _____ Award
                              NOUN

Darryl: _____ Award
               VERB ENDING IN "ING"

Oscar: Worst Salesman of the _____ Award
                                      NOUN

MAD LIBS® is fun to play with friends, but you can also play it by yourself! To begin with, DO NOT look at the story on the page below. Fill in the blanks on this page with the words called for. Then, using the words you have selected, fill in the blank spaces in the story.

Now you've created your own hilarious MAD LIBS® game!

HOME BEET HOME

A PLACE _____

NOUN _____

TYPE OF FOOD (PLURAL) _____

SAME TYPE OF FOOD (PLURAL) _____

VERB (PAST TENSE) _____

NOUN _____

PERSON IN ROOM _____

VERB _____

PART OF THE BODY _____

ADJECTIVE _____

TYPE OF BUILDING _____

NOUN _____

TYPE OF FOOD _____

CELEBRITY _____

NOUN _____

SAME NOUN _____

MAD LIBS®

HOME BEET HOME

One time, Jim and Pam spent the night at Dwight's beet

_____ , which was also a/an _____ -and-breakfast
A PLACE   NOUN

hotel. But they called it "the _____ Hotel" or "the
                                TYPE OF FOOD (PLURAL)

Embassy _____"! Once they _____
         SAME TYPE OF FOOD (PLURAL)   VERB (PAST TENSE)

into the _____ -room, Jim had this to say:
          NOUN

"You know, I just realized this is _____ 's and my first night
                                   PERSON IN ROOM

away together. I used to _____ it over in my _____ ,
                          VERB   PART OF THE BODY

and it was just a little bit different. Maybe a/an, ah, _____
                                                        ADJECTIVE

_____ or a romantic _____ . Wine, but wine
TYPE OF BUILDING   NOUN

that isn't made out of _____ . Didn't think _____
                        TYPE OF FOOD   CELEBRITY

would be involved at all. And ah, I always imagined less _____ .
                                                          NOUN

I mean, some _____ . Just less."
              SAME NOUN

MAD LIBS® is fun to play with friends, but you can also play it by yourself! To begin with, DO NOT look at the story on the page below. Fill in the blanks on this page with the words called for. Then, using the words you have selected, fill in the blank spaces in the story.

Now you've created your own hilarious MAD LIBS® game!

SNOWBALLS

NOUN _____

PERSON IN ROOM _____

CELEBRITY _____

VERB ENDING IN "ING" _____

NOUN _____

PART OF THE BODY _____

VERB _____

NOUN _____

ADJECTIVE _____

VERB ENDING IN "ING" _____

ADJECTIVE _____

NOUN _____

ADJECTIVE _____

ADJECTIVE _____

PLURAL NOUN _____

MAD LIBS

SNOWBALLS

When Dwight and Jim get in a snowball fight that ends up breaking

a/an _____ , they get counseled by Michael and
<u>NOUN</u>

_____ . Here's their conversation:
<u>PERSON IN ROOM</u>

Michael: What if _____ was taking her _____
<u>CELEBRITY</u> <u>VERB ENDING IN "ING"</u>

break below that window. You know what would have happened? The

shards of _____ would have shaved her _____
<u>NOUN</u> <u>PART OF THE BODY</u>

right off.

Dwight: I could not _____ more. I just want to state for the
<u>VERB</u>

_____ that I am intending to sue Jim for _____
<u>NOUN</u> <u>ADJECTIVE</u>

psychological distress.

Jim: What are you talking about? You're the one _____
<u>VERB ENDING IN "ING"</u>

me.

Dwight: With snowballs, Jim. _____ little
<u>ADJECTIVE</u>

_____ -balls.
<u>NOUN</u>

Holly: Dwight's _____ . What you did was dangerous and
<u>ADJECTIVE</u>

_____ . I'm really surprised at you guys. Last time I was here,
<u>ADJECTIVE</u>

you were both best _____ .
<u>PLURAL NOUN</u>

MAD LIBS® is fun to play with friends, but you can also play it by yourself! To begin with, DO NOT look at the story on the page below. Fill in the blanks on this page with the words called for. Then, using the words you have selected, fill in the blank spaces in the story.

Now you've created your own hilarious MAD LIBS® game!

IT ALL STARTS WITH AN IDEA

VERB _____

OCCUPATION _____

VEHICLE (PLURAL) _____

NOUN _____

VERB ENDING IN "S" _____

NOUN _____

VERB _____

NOUN _____

ADVERB _____

PLURAL NOUN _____

ADJECTIVE _____

VERB ENDING IN "S" _____

VERB _____

NOUN _____

VERB _____

LAST NAME _____

NOUN _____

MAD LIBS®
IT ALL STARTS
WITH AN IDEA

When it came time to film a commercial for the company, Michael

knew what he wanted to _____ . Here's the script from the
                          VERB

_____ 's cut of his Dunder Mifflin TV ad:
OCCUPATION

(Cue music from the movie _____ of _____)
                          VEHICLE (PLURAL)   NOUN

"It all _____ with an idea. But you can never tell where
        VERB ENDING IN "S"

a/an _____ will end up. Because ideas _____ , they
      NOUN   VERB

change, grow. They connect us with the _____ . And in a/an
                                          NOUN

_____ -moving world, where good _____ move
ADVERB   PLURAL NOUN

at the speed of time. And _____ news isn't always what it
                            ADJECTIVE

_____ . Because when push comes to _____ ,
VERB ENDING IN "S"   VERB

we all deserve a second _____ . . . to _____ .
                          NOUN   VERB

_____ Mifflin, limitless paper in a/an _____ -less
LAST NAME   NOUN

world."

MAD LIBS® is fun to play with friends, but you can also play it by yourself! To begin with, DO NOT look at the story on the page below. Fill in the blanks on this page with the words called for. Then, using the words you have selected, fill in the blank spaces in the story.

Now you've created your own hilarious MAD LIBS® game!

PRETZEL DAY

PLURAL NOUN _____

TYPE OF FOOD _____

A PLACE _____

VERB _____

VERB (PAST TENSE) _____

NOUN _____

EXCLAMATION _____

VERB ENDING IN "ING" _____

NOUN _____

ADJECTIVE _____

PLURAL NOUN _____

PERSON IN ROOM _____

PLURAL NOUN _____

VERB _____

TYPE OF BUILDING _____

NOUN _____

MAD LIBS

PRETZEL DAY

When Michael orders all of the _____ for his pretzel, he
PLURAL NOUN

ends up having a/an _____ rush in his _____ that
TYPE OF FOOD · A PLACE

makes him want to _____ everything about the whole
VERB

company. Here's the sugar-_____ rant he announced to
VERB (PAST TENSE)

everyone before collapsing on his _____:
NOUN

"Oh, _____, everyone! I am officially _____
EXCLAMATION · VERB ENDING IN "ING"

the efficiency of this _____. Second, I am insisting on
NOUN

_____ accountability from every single one of you. And I
ADJECTIVE

will be taking _____. Phyllis and _____, I want
PLURAL NOUN · PERSON IN ROOM

to you switch _____. I'm going to _____ the
PLURAL NOUN · VERB

physical structure of the _____ to maximize everything.
TYPE OF BUILDING

I think we're getting a lot done. Don't you? On paper, at least. And we

are, after all, a/an _____ company. Are we not? Are we not?
NOUN

Are we not? Are you with me? Are you with me? Thank you very

much!"

MAD LIBS® is fun to play with friends, but you can also play it by yourself! To begin with, DO NOT look at the story on the page below. Fill in the blanks on this page with the words called for. Then, using the words you have selected, fill in the blank spaces in the story.

Now you've created your own hilarious MAD LIBS® game!

STANLEY'S LIGHTHOUSE

PLURAL NOUN _____

OCCUPATION (PLURAL) _____

LAST NAME _____

FIRST NAME _____

ADJECTIVE _____

SAME FIRST NAME _____

ADJECTIVE _____

NOUN _____

TYPE OF BUILDING _____

VERB _____

VERB _____

NOUN _____

SAME TYPE OF BUILDING _____

NOUN _____

NUMBER _____

VERB _____

MAD LIBS®

STANLEY'S LIGHTHOUSE

Everyone has _____ and dreams! Even the
                            PLURAL NOUN

_____ who work at Dunder _____. And
OCCUPATION (PLURAL)   LAST NAME

_____ has the most _____ imagination of all.
FIRST NAME   ADJECTIVE

Here's _____'s _____ dream for the future:
       SAME FIRST NAME   ADJECTIVE

"Yes, I have a/an _____. And it's not some MLK dream
                   NOUN

for equality. I want to own a decommissioned _____.
                                              TYPE OF BUILDING

And I want to _____ at the top. And nobody knows I
               VERB

_____ there. And there's a/an _____ that I can
VERB   NOUN

press and launch that _____ into space."
                      SAME TYPE OF BUILDING

Let's hope his _____ comes true! Three, _____,
               NOUN   NUMBER

one . . . _____ -off!
          VERB

MAD LIBS® is fun to play with friends, but you can also play it by yourself! To begin with, DO NOT look at the story on the page below. Fill in the blanks on this page with the words called for. Then, using the words you have selected, fill in the blank spaces in the story.

Now you've created your own hilarious MAD LIBS® game!

OFFICE OLYMPICS

ADJECTIVE _____

VERB ENDING IN "ING" _____

TYPE OF BUILDING _____

NOUN _____

A PLACE _____

ADJECTIVE _____

NOUN _____

TYPE OF BUILDING _____

SILLY WORD _____

SAME SILLY WORD _____

SAME SILLY WORD _____

VERB _____

VERB ENDING IN "ING" _____

EXCLAMATION _____

COLOR _____

TYPE OF FOOD _____

PLURAL NOUN _____

The announcement of the first Dunder Mifflin Office Olympiad was

a/an _____ deal. While Michael and Dwight were out
　　　　ADJECTIVE

_____ Michael's first _____, the
VERB ENDING IN "ING"　　　　　　　　TYPE OF BUILDING

staff made a huge _____ that went across the whole
　　　　　　　　　　　NOUN

_____. To make the announcement of the event sound
A PLACE

more _____, Jim hummed the Olympic theme song and
　　　ADJECTIVE

made his own _____ effects by repeating the last part of
　　　　　　　NOUN

each sentence, so it seemed like they were all standing in a huge

_____. Here's his speech:
TYPE OF BUILDING

" _____ , _____ , _____ . . . This scented
　SILLY WORD　　SAME SILLY WORD　SAME SILLY WORD

candle-andle-andle, which I found in the men's _____
　　　　　　　　　　　　　　　　　　　　　　　VERB

-room-room-room represents the eternal _____ of
　　　　　　　　　　　　　　　　VERB ENDING IN "ING"

competition . . . or something. _____! We will be competing
　　　　　　　　　　　　　　EXCLAMATION

for _____, silver, and bronze _____ lids. Let the
　　COLOR　　　　　　　　　　　　TYPE OF FOOD

_____ begin!"
PLURAL NOUN

MAD LIBS® is fun to play with friends, but you can also play it by yourself! To begin with, DO NOT look at the story on the page below. Fill in the blanks on this page with the words called for. Then, using the words you have selected, fill in the blank spaces in the story.

Now you've created your own hilarious MAD LIBS® game!

THE FINER THINGS CLUB

ADJECTIVE _____

PLURAL NOUN _____

CELEBRITY _____

TYPE OF LIQUID _____

PLURAL NOUN _____

VERB ENDING IN "ING" _____

NOUN _____

PERSON IN ROOM _____

VERB ENDING IN "ING" _____

PLURAL NOUN _____

VERB _____

PLURAL NOUN _____

VERB _____

ADJECTIVE _____

ADJECTIVE _____

ADJECTIVE _____

NOUN _____

NOUN _____

THE FINER THINGS CLUB

Pam loves being a member of the _____ Things Club. It
                                    ADJECTIVE

gives her the chance to listen to classic _____ by composers
                                              PLURAL NOUN

like _____ and to sip _____ while discussing
        CELEBRITY   TYPE OF LIQUID

the deeper meanings found in classic _____ . Too bad the
                                         PLURAL NOUN

club's table is near the office _____ machine and the
                                   VERB ENDING IN "ING"

microwave _____ . Here's her description of the club:
               NOUN

"Oscar, _____ , and I are the _____
           PERSON IN ROOM   VERB ENDING IN "ING"

members of the Finer _____ Club. We _____ once
                         PLURAL NOUN   VERB

a month to discuss _____ and art and to _____
                        PLURAL NOUN   VERB

culture in a very _____ way. Sometimes the debate can get
                       ADJECTIVE

_____ . But we're always _____ . There is no
     ADJECTIVE   ADJECTIVE

_____ , no plastic, and no _____ talk allowed. It's
     NOUN   NOUN

very exclusive."

MAD LIBS® is fun to play with friends, but you can also play it by yourself! To begin with, DO NOT look at the story on the page below. Fill in the blanks on this page with the words called for. Then, using the words you have selected, fill in the blank spaces in the story.

Now you've created your own hilarious MAD LIBS® game!

BREAKFAST IN BED

ADJECTIVE _____

VERB (PAST TENSE) _____

VERB ENDING IN "ING" _____

TYPE OF FOOD _____

VERB _____

OCCUPATION _____

VERB _____

NUMBER _____

CELEBRITY _____

VERB _____

NOUN _____

VERB ENDING IN "ING" _____

ADJECTIVE _____

NOUN _____

NOUN _____

PART OF THE BODY _____

VERB _____

The Office US

MAD LIBS®

BREAKFAST IN BED

Michael loves breakfast! But sometimes breakfast can be _____ .
                                                              ADJECTIVE

Let's hear him tell us the story of how he _____ himself
                                           VERB (PAST TENSE)

while making breakfast:

"I enjoy _____ breakfast in bed. I like waking up to
          VERB ENDING IN "ING"

the smell of _____ . _____ me. And since I don't
              TYPE OF FOOD   VERB

have a/an _____ , I have to _____ it myself. So,
           OCCUPATION   VERB

most nights before I go to bed, I will lay _____ strips of bacon
                                            NUMBER

out on my _____ Grill. Then I go to sleep. When I wake up,
           CELEBRITY

I _____ in the _____ . I go back to sleep again.
   VERB   NOUN

Then I wake up to the smell of _____ bacon. It is
                                VERB ENDING IN "ING"

_____ . It's good for me. It's the perfect way to start the
 ADJECTIVE

_____ . Today, I got up, I stepped onto the _____ ,
 NOUN   NOUN

and it clamped down on my _____ . That's it. I don't see
                           PART OF THE BODY

what's so hard to _____ about that."
                   VERB

MAD LIBS® is fun to play with friends, but you can also play it by yourself! To begin with, DO NOT look at the story on the page below. Fill in the blanks on this page with the words called for. Then, using the words you have selected, fill in the blank spaces in the story.

Now you've created your own hilarious MAD LIBS® game!

JIM'S TOAST

NUMBER _____

NOUN _____

NOUN _____

VERB _____

VERB (PAST TENSE) _____

PERSON IN ROOM _____

PLURAL NOUN _____

VERB _____

NOUN _____

VERB ENDING IN "ING" _____

ADJECTIVE _____

ADJECTIVE _____

PLURAL NOUN _____

ADJECTIVE _____

VERB (PAST TENSE) _____

NOUN _____

TYPE OF FOOD _____

MAD LIBS®

JIM'S TOAST

_____ years ago, I was just a/an _____ who had
NUMBER   NOUN

a crush on a/an _____ who had a boyfriend. And I had to
NOUN

do the hardest thing that I've ever had to do, which was just to

_____ . Don't get me wrong, I _____ with her.
VERB   VERB (PAST TENSE)

_____ , I can now admit in front of _____
PERSON IN ROOM   PLURAL NOUN

and family that I do know how to _____ a photocopy . . .
VERB

didn't need your _____ that many times. And uh, do you
NOUN

remember how long it took you to teach me how to drive stick? I've

been _____ stick since _____ school. For
VERB ENDING IN "ING"   ADJECTIVE

a really _____ time, that's all I had. I just had little
ADJECTIVE

_____ with a girl who saw me as a friend. And a lot of
PLURAL NOUN

people told me I was _____ to wait this long for a date with
ADJECTIVE

a girl that I _____ with. But I think even then I knew
VERB (PAST TENSE)

that I was waiting for my _____ . So, I would like to propose
NOUN

a/an _____ !
TYPE OF FOOD

MAD LIBS® is fun to play with friends, but you can also play it by yourself! To begin with, DO NOT look at the story on the page below. Fill in the blanks on this page with the words called for. Then, using the words you have selected, fill in the blank spaces in the story.

Now you've created your own hilarious MAD LIBS® game!

THE ELECTRIC CITY

A PLACE _____

TYPE OF FOOD _____

NOUN _____

CELEBRITY _____

ADJECTIVE _____

NOUN _____

CITY _____

VERB _____

NOUN _____

PLURAL NOUN _____

VERB (PAST TENSE) _____

NOUN _____

VERB ENDING IN "ING" _____

VEHICLE (PLURAL) _____

ADJECTIVE _____

NOUN _____

PART OF THE BODY _____

ADJECTIVE _____

Dwight and Michael are working on some lyrics for their music video.

Check them out:

Sittin' in my _____ with a plate of grilled _____,
A PLACE · TYPE OF FOOD

called my _____ Dwight, just to see what was shakin'.
NOUN

Yo, _____, our town is _____ and pretty,
CELEBRITY · ADJECTIVE

so check out how we _____ in the Electric City!
NOUN

Lazy _____, the Electric City!
CITY

They _____ it that 'cause of the electri-city!
VERB

The city's laid out from _____ to west,
NOUN

and our public _____ and libraries are truly the best!
PLURAL NOUN

Call poison control if you're _____ by a spider,
VERB (PAST TENSE)

but check that it's covered by your _____ provider!
NOUN

Plenty of space in the _____ lot,
VERB ENDING IN "ING"

but the little _____ go in the _____ spot!
VEHICLE (PLURAL) · ADJECTIVE

_____ attack time, don't lose your _____,
NOUN · PART OF THE BODY

we like Cugino's for the _____ bread!
ADJECTIVE

MAD LIBS® is fun to play with friends, but you can also play it by yourself! To begin with, DO NOT look at the story on the page below. Fill in the blanks on this page with the words called for. Then, using the words you have selected, fill in the blank spaces in the story.

Now you've created your own hilarious MAD LIBS® game!

WHO'S YOUR WORM GUY?

ADJECTIVE _____

VERB _____

EXCLAMATION _____

A PLACE _____

VERB _____

NOUN _____

LETTER OF THE ALPHABET _____

PERSON IN ROOM _____

VERB _____

VERB ENDING IN "ING" _____

NOUN _____

ADJECTIVE _____

NOUN _____

VERB (PAST TENSE) _____

ADJECTIVE _____

PART OF THE BODY _____

NUMBER _____

MAD LIBS®

WHO'S YOUR WORM GUY?

Creed always seems to have something _____ to say, no
ADJECTIVE

matter the occasion. Let's _____ out some of his best!
VERB

- _____, man! I live by (the) _____. We should
EXCLAMATION   A PLACE

    hang out by the quarry and _____ things down there.
VERB

- I already won the _____, I was born in the US of
NOUN

    _____, baby.
LETTER OF THE ALPHABET

- Did one of you tell _____ that I have asthma? 'Cause
PERSON IN ROOM

    I don't. If this gets out they won't let me _____. If I
VERB

    can't scuba, what am I _____ toward?
VERB ENDING IN "ING"

- I wanna do a/an _____. But real _____-like.
NOUN   ADJECTIVE

    Not enough to make a big _____ out of it, but I know
NOUN

    everyone _____ it. One stunning, _____
VERB (PAST TENSE)   ADJECTIVE

    cartwheel.

- You ever seen a/an _____ with _____ toes?
PART OF THE BODY   NUMBER

MAD LIBS® is fun to play with friends, but you can also play it by yourself! To begin with, DO NOT look at the story on the page below. Fill in the blanks on this page with the words called for. Then, using the words you have selected, fill in the blank spaces in the story.

Now you've created your own hilarious MAD LIBS® game!

KELLY AND JIM
TALK ABOUT RYAN

CELEBRITY _____

ADVERB _____

ADJECTIVE _____

ADJECTIVE _____

A PLACE _____

PLURAL NOUN _____

NOUN _____

PART OF THE BODY _____

VERB (PAST TENSE) _____

VERB _____

VERB _____

EXCLAMATION _____

ADJECTIVE _____

PERSON IN ROOM _____

ADJECTIVE _____

ADVERB _____

NOUN _____

Kelly: Oh my god, Jim, last night, _____ and I totally,
CELEBRITY

_____ , hooked up. It was _____!
ADVERB   ADJECTIVE

Jim: Oh, that's great. I'm really _____ for you.
ADJECTIVE

Kelly: I know, and it was so funny, because we were at this

_____ with his _____ , and I was sitting next to
A PLACE   PLURAL NOUN

him the whole night. And he wasn't making a/an _____ , so
NOUN

in my _____ I was like "Ryan, what's taking you so long?"
PART OF THE BODY

And then, he _____ me, and I didn't know what to
VERB (PAST TENSE)

_____ . So I said, "Ryan, what took you so long?" I mean I
VERB

just said it to him, can you _____ that?
VERB

Jim: _____ .
EXCLAMATION

Kelly: Oh my god, Jim, is that _____ ? I'm embarrassed.
ADJECTIVE

Jim: No, don't be.

Kelly: Oh, thank _____ , because I was _____ ,
PERSON IN ROOM   ADJECTIVE

Jim, you would not believe. I was _____ nervous. But now—
ADVERB

now I have a/an _____ -friend!
NOUN

MAD LIBS® is fun to play with friends, but you can also play it by yourself! To begin with, DO NOT look at the story on the page below. Fill in the blanks on this page with the words called for. Then, using the words you have selected, fill in the blank spaces in the story.

Now you've created your own hilarious MAD LIBS® game!

CASUAL FRIDAY

PERSON IN ROOM _____

ADVERB _____

NOUN _____

NOUN _____

VERB ENDING IN "ING" _____

ADJECTIVE _____

PLURAL NOUN _____

CELEBRITY _____

VERB _____

ARTICLE OF CLOTHING (PLURAL) _____

ADVERB _____

COLOR _____

PART OF THE BODY _____

PART OF THE BODY (PLURAL) _____

PERSON IN ROOM _____

EXCLAMATION _____

ARTICLE OF CLOTHING (PLURAL) _____

ADJECTIVE _____

MAD LIBS®

CASUAL FRIDAY

Toby: Hey, _____ , can I talk to you _____ for a
PERSON IN ROOM   ADVERB

second?

Meredith: About what?

Toby: Your _____ .
NOUN

Meredith: What's wrong with my _____ ?
NOUN

Toby: You might consider _____ it down a touch. It's
VERB ENDING IN "ING"

riding up a little _____ .
ADJECTIVE

Meredith: A bunch of _____ . You know, _____'s
PLURAL NOUN   CELEBRITY

allowed to wear sandals, but I'm not allowed to _____ open-
VERB

toed _____ ?
ARTICLE OF CLOTHING (PLURAL)

(Meredith _____ pulls down her _____ dress!)
ADVERB   COLOR

Oscar: Meredith, your _____ is out!
PART OF THE BODY

(Meredith rolls her _____ and fixes her dress.)
PART OF THE BODY (PLURAL)

_____ : Too far, Meredith, too far!
PERSON IN ROOM

Kelly: _____ , Meredith! Where are your
EXCLAMATION

_____ ?
ARTICLE OF CLOTHING (PLURAL)

Meredith: It's _____ Day! Happy?
ADJECTIVE

MAD LIBS® is fun to play with friends, but you can also play it by yourself! To begin with, DO NOT look at the story on the page below. Fill in the blanks on this page with the words called for. Then, using the words you have selected, fill in the blank spaces in the story.

Now you've created your own hilarious MAD LIBS® game!

PHYLLIS'S RAINY DAY

ANIMAL (PLURAL) _____

EXCLAMATION _____

VERB _____

NOUN _____

ADJECTIVE _____

NOUN _____

PLURAL NOUN _____

ADJECTIVE _____

VERB _____

SOMETHING ALIVE (PLURAL) _____

NOUN _____

ADVERB _____

VERB ENDING IN "ING" _____

VERB _____

NOUN _____

ADJECTIVE _____

ADJECTIVE _____

TYPE OF BUILDING _____

MAD LIBS®

PHYLLIS'S RAINY DAY

Wow, it is raining _____ and dogs out there.
<u>ANIMAL (PLURAL)</u>

_____! I just _____ it when it rains; this is my
<u>EXCLAMATION</u>   <u>VERB</u>

favorite kind of _____ . The only _____ part about
<u>NOUN</u>   <u>ADJECTIVE</u>

rainy days is that nobody knows how to drive in the _____ .
<u>NOUN</u>

You know, the _____ are actually the slickest in the first
<u>PLURAL NOUN</u>

half hour. But the _____ driving conditions are worth it
<u>ADJECTIVE</u>

for all the other joys the rain can _____ . Like, for example,
<u>VERB</u>

the plants—oh, the _____ are going to love this
<u>SOMETHING ALIVE (PLURAL)</u>

weather. Plus, lots of things are so cozy in the _____ . And
<u>NOUN</u>

I actually sleep _____ when it's _____ .
<u>ADVERB</u>   <u>VERB ENDING IN "ING"</u>

Normally the rain would make me want to _____ at home,
<u>VERB</u>

curled up with a good _____ , but everybody's being so
<u>NOUN</u>

_____ to me today. They keep coming up to me to chat,
<u>ADJECTIVE</u>

which is so _____ . I'm really happy being here in the
<u>ADJECTIVE</u>

_____ today!
<u>TYPE OF BUILDING</u>

MAD LIBS® is fun to play with friends, but you can also play it by yourself! To begin with, DO NOT look at the story on the page below. Fill in the blanks on this page with the words called for. Then, using the words you have selected, fill in the blank spaces in the story.

Now you've created your own hilarious MAD LIBS® game!

WAREHOUSE BASKETBALL

ADJECTIVE _____

NOUN _____

VERB ENDING IN "ING" _____

NOUN _____

NOUN _____

FIRST NAME _____

NOUN _____

NOUN _____

VERB _____

PART OF THE BODY _____

SILLY WORD _____

NOUN _____

SILLY WORD _____

NOUN _____

SILLY WORD _____

PLURAL NOUN _____

VERB _____

NOUN _____

MAD LIBS®

WAREHOUSE BASKETBALL

Michael lays out his _____ feelings about the game of
                          ADJECTIVE

_____-ball:
      NOUN

"When I am _____ hoops, all of the stress and
              VERB ENDING IN "ING"

_____ of my job here just melt away. It's gone. I'm in the
      NOUN

_____. Who am I? Am I _____ Scott? I don't
      NOUN   FIRST NAME

know. I might just be a/an _____ machine. What's Dunder
                                NOUN

Mifflin? I've never heard of it. Filing _____? Who cares?
                                              NOUN

Possible downsizing? Well . . . um . . . that's probably going to

_____ actually. _____-ball is like rock and roll.
      VERB   PART OF THE BODY

It's just _____. And basketball is like _____, you
            SILLY WORD   NOUN

know? You're kind of _____. It's all downbeat, it's in the
                          SILLY WORD

_____, it's like _____. The great thing about
      NOUN   SILLY WORD

_____ is that it is all about character. And you can
      PLURAL NOUN

_____ lessons about _____ even if you don't win.
      VERB   NOUN

But we did because we were ahead."

MAD LIBS® is fun to play with friends, but you can also play it by yourself! To begin with, DO NOT look at the story on the page below. Fill in the blanks on this page with the words called for. Then, using the words you have selected, fill in the blank spaces in the story.

Now you've created your own hilarious MAD LIBS® game!

BOOM! ROASTED!

SILLY WORD _____

PLURAL NOUN _____

NOUN _____

VERB _____

ANIMAL _____

TYPE OF BUILDING _____

PERSON IN ROOM _____

SILLY WORD _____

NOUN _____

TYPE OF FOOD _____

NOUN _____

LAST NAME _____

NUMBER _____

CELEBRITY _____

VERB _____

TYPE OF FOOD _____

MAD LIBS®

BOOM! ROASTED!

The Dunder _____ office loves nothing more than roasting
          SILLY WORD

one another! Here's the list of some of the best _____:
                                                  PLURAL NOUN

- **Kelly:** I have made a/an _____ of people I would make
                          NOUN

  out with before I would _____ out with Michael Scott:
                          VERB

  a/an _____, a fridge, anybody from the
                    ANIMAL

  _____, a wood chipper, _____, a candle,
    TYPE OF BUILDING   PERSON IN ROOM

  and Lord _____.
            SILLY WORD

- **Michael:** Angela? Where's Angela? Whoa, there you are, I didn't see

  you behind that _____ of _____.
                  NOUN   TYPE OF FOOD

- **Pam:** Once every hour someone is involved in an internet

  _____. That man is Michael _____.
    NOUN   LAST NAME

- **Michael:** Jim, you're 6'11" and you weigh _____
                                              NUMBER

  pounds—_____ has a better body than you.
            CELEBRITY

- **Andy:** What I hate about you, you really _____ as a
                                            VERB

  boss. You're the losiest, jerkiest, and you're dumber than

  _____-sauce.
    TYPE OF FOOD

MAD LIBS® is fun to play with friends, but you can also play it by yourself! To begin with, DO NOT look at the story on the page below. Fill in the blanks on this page with the words called for. Then, using the words you have selected, fill in the blank spaces in the story.

Now you've created your own hilarious MAD LIBS® game!

DWIGHT'S BIG SPEECH

PLURAL NOUN _____

NOUN _____

VERB ENDING IN "ING" _____

NOUN _____

NOUN _____

ADJECTIVE _____

ADJECTIVE _____

VERB _____

OCCUPATION (PLURAL) _____

VERB _____

NOUN _____

ADJECTIVE _____

PLURAL NOUN _____

NOUN _____

VERB _____

VERB _____

MAD LIBS®

DWIGHT'S BIG SPEECH

Blood alone moves the _____ of history! Have you ever
PLURAL NOUN

asked yourselves in an hour of _____ , which everyone
NOUN

finds during the day, how long we have been _____
VERB ENDING IN "ING"

for greatness? Not only the years we've been at war, the war of

_____ , but from the moment as a child when we realized
NOUN

that the _____ could be conquered. It has been a/an
NOUN

_____ struggle. A/An _____ fight. I say to you,
ADJECTIVE   ADJECTIVE

and you will understand that it is a privilege to _____! We
VERB

are warriors! _____ of northeastern Pennsylvania, I ask
OCCUPATION (PLURAL)

you once more: _____ and be worthy of this historical hour!
VERB

No _____ is worth anything if it cannot defend itself!
NOUN

Some people will tell you "salesman" is a/an _____ word.
ADJECTIVE

They'll conjure up images of used-car dealers and door-to-door

_____ . This is our duty: to change their _____ . I
PLURAL NOUN   NOUN

say salesmen . . . and women of the world, _____! We must
VERB

never acquiesce for it is together, TOGETHER, THAT WE PREVAIL!

We must never _____ control of the motherland!
VERB

MAD LIBS® is fun to play with friends, but you can also play it by yourself! To begin with, DO NOT look at the story on the page below. Fill in the blanks on this page with the words called for. Then, using the words you have selected, fill in the blank spaces in the story.

Now you've created your own hilarious MAD LIBS® game!

THE BEST OF THE PPC

VERB ENDING IN "ING" _____

ADJECTIVE _____

NOUN _____

ADJECTIVE _____

ADJECTIVE _____

NOUN _____

COUNTRY _____

ADJECTIVE _____

PERSON IN ROOM _____

VERB _____

ANIMAL _____

NOUN _____

COLOR _____

VERB ENDING IN "ING" _____

CELEBRITY _____

ADJECTIVE _____

The Party _____ Committee had quite a history within
<u>VERB ENDING IN "ING"</u>

the office, but one of the most _____ parties was the
<u>ADJECTIVE</u>

Moroccan Christmas _____ when Phyllis was in charge.
<u>NOUN</u>

Phyllis had a lot of _____ thoughts about it:
<u>ADJECTIVE</u>

"This is the _____ Christmas Party I'm throwing as head of
<u>ADJECTIVE</u>

the Party Planning _____. The theme is Night in
<u>NOUN</u>

_____. This isn't your grandmother's Christmas party.
<u>COUNTRY</u>

Unless, of course, she's from Morocco, in which case it's very

_____. For example, when _____ tried to
<u>ADJECTIVE</u>   <u>PERSON IN ROOM</u>

_____ the nativity scene, I told her it's not on theme. She
<u>VERB</u>

could keep her camel, _____, and elephant, and the
<u>ANIMAL</u>

North African _____ can stay, but everything else goes
<u>NOUN</u>

in the drawer. Why does she listen to me? Oh, I don't think it's

_____ -mail. Angela just does what I ask her to do so I won't
<u>COLOR</u>

tell everyone that she's _____ on Andy with
<u>VERB ENDING IN "ING"</u>

_____. I think for it to be blackmail, it would have to be
<u>CELEBRITY</u>

a/an _____ letter."
<u>ADJECTIVE</u>

Download Mad Libs today!

Join the millions of Mad Libs fans
creating wacky and wonderful
stories on our apps!